T0065750

# ABRAHAM

## MODEL OF FAITH

12 Studies for Individuals or Groups

J A M E S   R E A P S O M E

**FISHERMAN**
BIBLE STUDYGUIDES

ABRAHAM
A SHAW BOOK
PUBLISHED BY WATERBROOK PRESS
12265 Oracle Boulevard, Suite 200
Colorado Springs, CO 80921
*A division of Random House, Inc.*

ISBN: 978-0-87788-003-5

146484122

# CONTENTS

# INTRODUCTION

Faith lies at the heart of God's message to us in the Bible. Strip the Bible of faith and you have very little left. God confronts his people with their duty to trust, love, and obey him. Yet, except for a skimpy definition in Hebrews 11:1, the Bible does not offer a lengthy theological treatise on faith. Rather, the writers go to great lengths to describe people of faith.

One such person of faith is the patriarch Abraham. We find his story not only in the book of Genesis, but throughout Scripture. He is one of many listed in the Hebrews 11 "Hall of Fame" of the faithful, and there he shines above the others. When we discover the critical meaning of saving faith in Romans 4, Abraham is our model again. This ought to tell us something about the importance and value of studying his life of faith.

But the narratives in Genesis do not exalt the man; they exalt his God. These studies will help us discover what kind of person Abraham was. At the same time, since faith is useless unless it rests on a rock solid foundation, we will also learn more about the God whom Abraham trusted. God was completely trustworthy, even though at times it seemed to Abraham that God had forgotten to keep his word. We shall also discover a God of grace and forgiveness when our hero of faith stumbled.

This study will also attempt to translate Abraham's battles for faith and obedience into meaning for our similar battles today. You will find many questions to help you focus on how Abraham's struggles can help you to grow stronger in faithful obedience to God. I pray that you will become as excited as I was when I studied the life of Abraham. He became known as "God's friend" (James 2:23)—a worthy aspiration for all of us.

James Reapsome

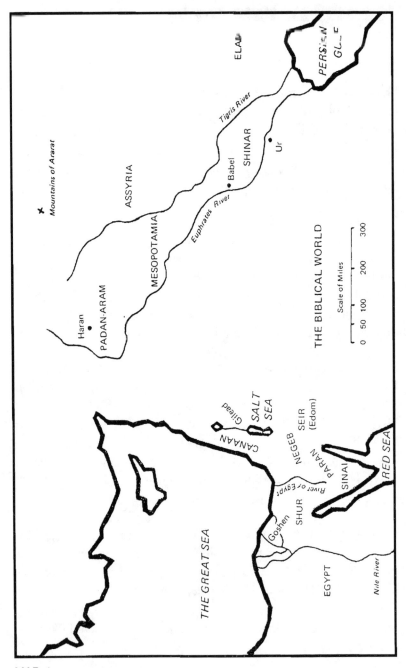

THE BIBLICAL WORLD

Scale of Miles

0  50  100      200      300

MAP 1

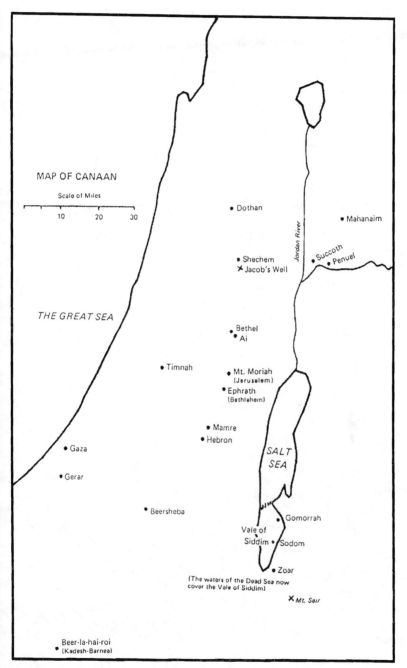

MAP OF CANAAN

Scale of Miles

10    20    30

• Dothan

• Mahanaim

Jordan River

• Shechem           • Succoth
✗ Jacob's Well        • Penuel

THE GREAT SEA

• Bethel
• Ai

• Timnah

• Mt. Moriah
  (Jerusalem)
• Ephrath
  (Bethlehem)

• Mamre
• Hebron

SALT
SEA

• Gaza

• Gerar

• Beersheba

• Gomorrah
Vale of
Siddim • • Sodom

• Zoar

(The waters of the Dead Sea now
cover the Vale of Siddim)

✗ Mt. Seir

Beer-la-hai-roi
• (Kadesh-Barnea)

MAP 2

# HOW TO USE THIS STUDYGUIDE

Fisherman studyguides are based on the inductive approach to Bible study. Inductive study is discovery study; we discover what the Bible says as we ask questions about its content and search for answers. This is quite different from the process in which a teacher *tells* a group *about* the Bible, what it means, and what to do about it. In inductive study, God speaks directly to each of us through his Word.

A group functions best when a leader keeps the discussion on target, but this leader is neither the teacher nor the "answer person." A leader's responsibility is to *ask*—not *tell*. The answers come from the text itself as group members examine, discuss, and think together about the passage.

There are four kinds of questions in each study. The first is an *approach question*. Used before the Bible passage is read, this question breaks the ice and helps you focus on the topic of the Bible study. It begins to reveal where thoughts and feelings need to be transformed by Scripture.

Some of the earlier questions in each study are *observation questions* designed to help you find out basic facts—who, what, where, when, and how.

When you know what the Bible says, you need to ask, *What does it mean?* These *interpretation questions* help you to discover the writer's basic message.

*Application questions* ask *What does it mean to me?* They challenge you to live out the Scripture's life-transforming message.

Fisherman studyguides provide spaces between questions for jotting down responses and related questions you would like to raise in the group. Each group member should have a copy of the studyguide and may take a turn in leading the group.

For consistency, Fisherman guides are written from the *New International Version*. But a group should feel free to use the NIV or any other accurate, modern translation of the Bible such as the *New Living Translation,* the *New Revised Standard Version,* the *New Jerusalem Bible,* or the *Good News Bible.* (Other paraphrases of the Bible may be referred to when additional help is needed.) Bible commentaries should not be brought to a Bible study because they tend to dampen discussion and keep people from thinking for themselves.

## SUGGESTIONS FOR GROUP LEADERS

**1.** Read and study the Bible passage thoroughly beforehand, grasping its themes and applying its teachings for yourself. Pray that the Holy Spirit will "guide you into truth" so that your leadership will guide others.

**2.** If the studyguide's questions ever seem ambiguous or unnatural to you, rephrase them, feeling free to add others that seem necessary to bring out the meaning of a verse.

**3.** Begin (and end) the study promptly. Start by asking someone to pray for God's help. Remember, the Holy Spirit is the teacher, not you!

**4.** Ask for volunteers to read the passages out loud.

**5.** As you ask the studyguide's questions in sequence, encourage everyone to participate in the discussion. If some are silent, ask,

"What do you think, Heather?" or "Dan, what can you add to that answer?" or suggest, "Let's have an answer from someone who hasn't spoken up yet."

**6.** If a question comes up that you can't answer, don't be afraid to admit that you're baffled! Assign the topic as a research project for someone to report on next week.

**7.** Keep the discussion moving and focused. Though tangents will inevitably be introduced, you can bring the discussion back to the topic at hand. Learn to pace the discussion so that you finish a study each session you meet.

**8.** Don't be afraid of silences; some questions take time to answer and some people need time to gather courage to speak. If silence persists, rephrase your question, but resist the temptation to answer it yourself.

**9.** If someone comes up with an answer that is clearly illogical or unbiblical, ask him or her for further clarification: "What verse suggests that to you?"

**10.** Discourage Bible-hopping and overuse of cross-references. Learn all you can from *this* passage, along with a few important references suggested in the studyguide.

**11.** Some questions are marked with a ♦. This indicates that further information is available in the Leader's Notes at the back of the guide.

**12.** For further information on getting a new Bible study group started and keeping it functioning effectively, read Gladys Hunt's *You Can Start a Bible Study Group* and *Pilgrims in Progress: Growing through Groups* by Jim and Carol Plueddemann.

## SUGGESTIONS FOR GROUP MEMBERS

**1.** Learn and apply the following ground rules for effective Bible study. (If new members join the group later, review these guidelines with the whole group.)

**2.** Remember that your goal is to learn all that you can *from the Bible passage being studied.* Let it speak for itself without using Bible commentaries or other Bible passages. There is more than enough in each assigned passage to keep your group productively occupied for one session. Sticking to the passage saves the group from insecurity and confusion.

**3.** Avoid the temptation to bring up those fascinating tangents that don't really grow out of the passage you are discussing. If the topic is of common interest, you can bring it up later in informal conversation following the study. Meanwhile, help each other stick to the subject!

**4.** Encourage each other to participate. People remember best what they discover and verbalize for themselves. Some people are naturally shier than others, or they may be afraid of making a mistake. If your discussion is free and friendly and you show real interest in what other group members think and feel, they will be more likely to speak up. Remember, the more people involved in a discussion, the richer it will be.

**5.** Guard yourself from answering too many questions or talking too much. Give others a chance to express themselves. If you are one who participates easily, discipline yourself by counting to ten before you open your mouth!

**6.** Make personal, honest applications and commit yourself to letting God's Word change you.

# A RADICAL CALL

Genesis 11:27–12:9

When we first meet Abraham, he is called Abram, "exalted father." A man of comfortable means, he is suddenly uprooted by a radical call from the Lord. God tears him from his civilized urban environment and makes him a wandering desert pilgrim. But even more radical is the promise God makes to Abram. In place of obscurity, God offers him greatness. However, to follow God's call costs Abram everything.

When God intervenes in our lives, the stakes are usually high. The salvation history of the Christian church can be traced back to this one man's decision to obey God's radical call. We see from Abram's life that each step of obedience to God leads to greater things.

**1.** Think about a time you or someone you know moved to a new city or changed jobs. In what ways did you experience God's guidance? How does God speak to us in these matters today?

14

♦ **2.** Abram's father, Terah, had left Ur for Canaan (11:31). Why do you suppose they settled in Haran instead?

**3.** What did God tell Abram to do (12:1)?

How would such a radical departure affect his life? His extended family (11:31 and 12:4-5)?

♦ **4.** How did God encourage Abram to follow him (12:2-3)?

What was the key to Abram's becoming the father of a great nation and the source of universal blessing?

**5.** As Abram pondered his journey into the unknown, what would he have considered necessary for success? Why?

**6.** How do God's promises surpass our needs and dreams?

**7.** What strikes you about Abram's response in 12:4?

Imagine the pros and cons Abram and Sarai may have discussed before they set out.

**8.** When change is required, what makes leaving one's friends or family or country so difficult?

Why is it sometimes necessary to leave them for the sake of Jesus and the Gospel? What happens when we fail to obey?

♦ **9.** What further promise did God give to Abram (verses 6-7)? Who already owned the land?

♦ **10.** Why do you think Abram worshiped God wherever he "pitched his tent" (verses 7-9)?

What might he have asked God for when he prayed?

**11.** Reviewing the passage, what was the short-range goal of Abram's faith and obedience?

How did that relate to his long-range destiny?

**12.** What steps of faith and obedience might God want you to take now? How do they fit your long-range dreams and expectations?

# UNEXPECTED ROADBLOCKS

Genesis 12:10-20; 13:1-18

When God called me to my first pastorate, I was excited. All the potential blessings thrilled me. But one day, shortly after I had said yes, serious doubts and fears began to assail me. Why had I agreed to do this? Was I really able to handle everything that goes with the pastor's job in addition to preaching? This was crazy; perhaps I should back out. But I didn't and I never regretted saying yes to God and his people.

When God said go, Abram went, but he immediately encountered serious trouble and faced considerable risks. He would not become a great man overnight.

1. When we obey God's voice, we sometimes encounter serious roadblocks. Why doesn't God make it easy to follow him?

**Read Genesis 12:10-20.**

◆ **2.** Why did Abram leave Canaan for Egypt?


Was this decision a failure of his faith? Why or why not?


◆ **3.** What did Abram fear, and how did he propose to handle it (verses 11-13)?


How do you account for his deception?


**4.** What worked about Abram's strategy? What didn't work?


**5.** How did God bail him out? Why do you think God rescued him?

**6.** In what situations are you likely to forsake your trust in God?

How have God's grace and mercy intervened in your life in those times?

---

**Read Genesis 13:1-18.**

**7.** Abram traveled back to Canaan. Contrast Abram's situation in Genesis 12:10 with his situation now (verses 2 and 6). What differences do you see?

♦ **8.** How did Abram's prosperity turn into a test of his faith (verses 5-9)?

Why is it often hard to love and obey God when things are going well for us?

◆ **9.** How do you account for Abram's generosity to Lot (verses 8-11)? Why didn't he take the better land he was entitled to?

**10.** What risks were involved in Lot's choice?

In what ways does our culture affect the exercise of our worship, faith, and obedience?

**11.** What new promise did God give Abram (verses 14-17)? Why? (Compare with Genesis 12:1-3).

◆ **12.** What still characterized Abram's life in Canaan (verses 3-4, 18)?

Why is worship the cornerstone of faith and obedience?

**13.** How can you trust God to take care of you when your earthly prospects seem dim, or when others seem to be "getting ahead" faster than you are?

# FAITH TAKES ACTION

Genesis 14

Popular gurus of success seminars tell us it's okay to look out for number one, to be a "winner," and to be as wealthy as you want to be. In this culture where selfishness is encouraged, making God-honoring choices is hard. Even two thousand years ago, Abram's faith was severely tested in regard to these notions of putting yourself first. Facing a tough situation with some of his family members, Abram had some difficult moral choices to make. Would he choose to bolster his own security or would he risk losing it? In these stories we find vivid evidence that faith must swing into action and take steps that may be contrary to conventional wisdom.

**1.** Sometimes family disputes boil to the surface and we are called to take sides. How do we decide whether or not to intervene?

24

---

**Read Genesis 14:1-10.**

◆ **2.** Find the area of the war of the kings on the map on page 7. How did the war affect Abram and Lot?

◆ **3.** Why do you think Abram decided to fight for his nephew?

What was Abram risking by taking this action?

**4.** What was the final outcome for Lot and his family (verse 16)? for Abram?

---

**Read Genesis 14:17-24.**

◆ **5.** What things do you learn about the man who came to Abram on his return (verses 17-18)?

---

♦ **6.** Summarize the blessing of Melchizedek (verses 19-20).

Why was this important for Abram?

**7.** Up to this point, God has been identified as simply the "Lord." What more does Abram learn about God?

♦ **8.** How did Abram respond to the priest's blessing? Why?

**9.** In New Testament terms, God has delivered us from the kingdom of sin, death, and darkness. What is our proper offering to him for his mercy? (See Romans 12:1; 1 Corinthians 6:20; 2 Corinthians 5:15.)

**10.** What offer did the king of Sodom make to Abram (verse 21)?

**11.** What was the motivation for Abram's answer?

Do you agree with his logic? Why or why not?

**12.** How was the king's offer a test of Abram's faith in God?

What kinds of offers, deals, and solicitations in our culture can subvert our faith?

**13.** Review the tests of Abram's faith so far in Genesis 12–14. How would you evaluate his record to this point?

How do you evaluate your walk of faith at this point in your life?

# ABRAM'S FAITH ENCOURAGED

Genesis 15

Abram had rescued Lot and his family and he had resisted the advances of a pagan king. He had been blessed by God's priest. But he was still childless and was feeling sorry for himself. According to Abram's thinking, time was running out for the possibility of an heir. In a dramatic encounter with the Lord, Abram learned that his obedience to God's call was just the first step. God's plan for him was embedded in a covenant—a promise—that Abram was forced to either reject or believe. Abram's faith had to be anchored in God himself; his hope had to be anchored in God's promise.

**1.** Why do we sometimes plunge into doubt or depression immediately after a time of spiritual success and material blessing?

Read Genesis 15:1-6.

**2.** What initial command did the Lord give to Abram (verse 1)? Why?

**3.** How did God portray himself to Abram (verse 1)?

How would these pictures speak to Abram's fears and needs? How do they speak to your fears and needs?

◆ **4.** What was Abram's problem and who did he blame for it (verses 2-3)?

What feelings lay under Abram's words?

◆ **5.** How did Abram propose to solve the situation?

What critical fact had he overlooked (verse 4)?

**6.** How did God encourage Abram's faith (verse 5)?

**7.** What is Abram's response to God's promise (verse 6)? Why?

What obstacles loomed in the way of his believing he would have physical descendants?

**8.** What are some things that often conspire to keep us from believing God's promises?

♦ **9.** God credited Abram's faith as "righteousness" (verse 6). Considering some of Abram's great accomplishments thus far, why do you think they did not count as righteousness?

**10.** Discuss ways people today think they can achieve righteousness before God.

What is the only way to such righteousness (see Romans 3:22)?

---

## Read Genesis 7-21.

**11.** What further concern did Abram reveal in verse 8? Why?

♦ **12.** In what dramatic way did God help him to believe in this case (verse 17-19)?

Why do you suppose God told Abram about the four hundred years of bondage in Egypt (verse 13)?

**13.** In what ways does this dialogue between God and Abram instruct you in your walk of faith?

# WHEN FAITH CAN'T WAIT

Genesis 16

We live in a hurry up culture. We demand fast relief for headaches and heartburn. We devour fast food and prepare instant meals. We grab cash from instant bank machines and wear out the "door close" button on elevators. Impatience robs our faith, too, of peace and contentment, and of seeing God's long-term perspective. Abram sometimes struggled with impatience. In this study, we see that he decided to do things his way when his faith could not wait for God's promises to be fulfilled.

**1.** How does our high energy, twenty-four hours a day, seven days a week tempo of life interfere with the life of faith?

Read Genesis 16:1-6.

♦ **2.** Since barrenness was a disgrace to women in Abram's day, what did Sarai propose to her husband (verse 2)? What was her reasoning?

**3.** Why do you think Abram agreed to go along with her plan?

**4.** What was the outcome of their plan for Abram? Sarai? and Hagar (verses 4-6)?

**5.** Of what sins was each one guilty?

Give your reasons for, and spiritual analysis of, this tragic mess.

♦ **6.** Why did Sarai blame Abram for her suffering (verse 5)?

How did Abram respond (verse 6)? Why?

**7.** Note how long Abram and Sarai had been waiting on God's promise (verse 3). Under what circumstances do you find it hard to wait for God? What makes it tough to keep on believing?

**8.** When family or relationship pressures mount, in what ways is your faith tested?

Why is mutual faith needed to avoid family disasters?

**Read Genesis 16:7-16.**

**9.** When Hagar the Egyptian started for home, God intervened. What did the angel of the Lord tell her (verses 9-12)?

◆ **10.** Imagine how you would have felt at this news. What was Hagar's response to the angel (or, the LORD) (verses 13-14)?

**11.** Who emerges as the person of faith in this story? Why?

**12.** How did God save Abram, despite his loss of trust?

**13.** What instruction and hope do you receive from this account?

# A NEW COVENANT

Genesis 17

Covenants—or contracts—are a part of everyday life. We shake hands on a verbal agreement with a neighbor. We use credit cards based on a contract, in very small print, with the card company. We all experience a variety of person-to-person convenantal relationships.

But God, in his wisdom, chose Abram to give the spectacular news of an agreement between the Almighty and one man and his descendants. Nothing like this had ever happened before in the history of the human race. God even gave Abram and his wife new names to emphasize the promise that, despite their advanced years, he would give them a son through whom the terms of the agreement would be fulfilled. Could Abram keep trusting God's promise?

**1.** What is one of the most promising covenants you have ever made? The most demanding? The scariest?

Read Genesis 17.1-14.

**2.** How many years have passed since Abram and Sarai took the problem of an heir into their own hands? (See Genesis 16:16 and 17:1).

♦ **3.** By what new name did God identify himself this time (verse 1)?

What was the significance of this name at this juncture in Abram's life?

**4.** What command did God give (verse 1)? Why?

How did Abram respond?

**5.** List the specific promises God made in this appearance (verses 2-8).

Did he reveal anything new to Abram? (Compare with Genesis 12:2-3, 7 and 13:14-16.)

◆ **6.** How did God's changing Abram's name help Abraham persevere in his walk of faith?

**7.** On what terms did God establish his covenant (contract or agreement) with Abraham (verses 9-14)? Compare this with Genesis 12:2-3 and 15:4-5. Describe the progress of God's self-revelation to Abraham and the consequences for him.

Looking back, what has God done for you over time to stabilize and develop your faith?

♦ 8. What was the outward sign that Abraham was a partner in God's covenant (verses 9-14)? Who was included in these terms?

**Read Genesis 17:15-27.**

9. Contrast Abram's response here with that of verse 3. How do you account for Abraham's laughter when God promised that Sarah would bear him a son (verses 17-18)?

Why did he cling to his hope that Ishmael might be his heir?

10. Through whom would God's covenant with Abraham be fulfilled (verses 19-21)? What would become of Ishmael's line?

♦ **11.** How did Abraham demonstrate his faith and his agreement with the terms of God's covenant (verses 23-27)?

**12.** When outward circumstances in your life seem to indicate that God's promises are not coming true, what recourse do you have?

**13.** Think through some of the promises of God given to believers in Christ. How do we know his Word is good? What is our duty in light of his promises?

# A BOLD PRAYER

Genesis 18

An old proverb says, "If you're skating on thin ice, you better have broad blades on your skates." In this study, we find Abraham and Sarah skating on some thin ice with God. Sarah shows her true colors in her own test of faith, while Abraham confronts God about the justice of his plans. Flinging questions to the Almighty, this bold dialogue with God shows Abraham's humanity in a new way, as well as his sure faith in the Judge of all the earth.

**1.** Dialogues with God can be either frightening or reassuring. Talk about a time in which you have questioned or dialogued with God. Was it reassuring or not? What made the difference for you?

**Read Genesis 18:1-15.**

♦ **2.** Who appeared to Abraham (verses 1-2, 10, 13)?

How do we know that he recognized the visitors as representing God?

**3.** What was the point of this visit, and what further development do we learn about God's plan (verse 10)?

**4.** To what obvious insurmountable human difficulty did the Lord address his question in verse 14?

How do you think Abraham would have answered his question? Why?

**5.** Why did Sarah's reaction change from laughter to lying?

**Read Genesis 18:16-33.**

♦ **6.** What brought Sodom and Gomorrah to God's attention (verses 20-21)?

How do we know the extent of sin among the people in these cities (verse 32)?

♦ **7.** Why did God choose to reveal his judgment of Sodom and Gomorrah to Abraham (verses 17-19)?

What does this tell us about their relationship?

**8.** Why do you think Abraham decided to intercede with God for these wicked cities (see Genesis 13:12-13)?

To what attributes of God did he appeal (verse 25)?

9. Describe Abraham's attitude as he approached the Lord (verses 27, 30-32)?

10. How did God later answer Abraham's bold prayer (see Genesis 19:29)?

11. As you reflect on the dialogue between God and Abraham, what qualities of faith and character in Abraham impress you? Why?

12. Contrast Abraham and Sarah in this chapter. How were Abraham's faith and leadership tested? With what outcomes?

13. Think about prayer as intercession. How should we pray for whole cities and countries? How can we grow the boldness of faith that Abraham displayed?

# A SON IS BORN

Genesis 21:1-21

The couple waits for nine months. Then phone calls, faxes, and e-mails carry the announcement around the world: "The baby has arrived! Mother and child are doing well." A new baby is always a welcome miracle, but imagine what it would be like if the father was one hundred years old, the mother ninety-one, and they had been waiting for years! Abraham and Sarah had much to celebrate as the good hand of the Lord blessed them. They had waited and waited through long years of God's repeated promises, and finally his word came true. Out of seemingly impossible circumstances, God's covenant fell into place.

**1.** In a day when having babies seems to have moved from the miraculous to the mechanical, how do we acknowledge the good hand of the Lord upon us?

Read Genesis 21.1-7.

♦ **2.** What characteristic of God did the writer emphasize (verses 1-2; see also Genesis 18:10, 14)? Why?

**3.** Imagine Sarah's thoughts during her pregnancy— about herself, God, and her husband. How do you think she prayed?

**4.** The name *Isaac* means "he laughs." Why was this an appropriate name for the child (see Genesis 17:17; 18:12, 15)?

**5.** In their joy, do you think Abraham and Sarah remembered laughing at God's prediction? To whom did Sarah give credit for her joy (verse 6)?

**6.** How do you think Abraham's household, friends, and surrounding people responded to Isaac's birth?

Do you think Abraham had talked to them about God's promises?

**7.** In what two ways did Abraham show his obedience to the Lord (verses 3-4; see also 17:19)? Why was this important?

**8.** The writer of Hebrews credits Abraham's faith for the birth of Isaac (Hebrews 11:11). How would you substantiate the writer's conclusion?

♦ **9.** How does this event enlarge your understanding of faith? Your views of God's character and his ways with his people?

Read Genesis 21:0-21.

♦ **10.** What facts did God remind Abraham of in order to put his mind at rest (verses 8-13)?

Why do you think God had to keep on telling him this?

♦ **11.** How did God test Abraham's faith and obedience (verse 14)?

How do you suppose Abraham felt when he sent Hagar and Ishmael into the desert?

**12.** Sarah's joy was marred by jealousy. Abraham's joy was marred by fear for his son Ishmael. What steps can you take to guard your spiritual integrity when feelings like these arise in your personal relationships?

# ABRAHAM'S SEVEREST TEST

Genesis 22:1-19

All of us have tasted the bitterness of life, but few have had to struggle with God's ways like Abraham did. He was asked to leave his homeland, to suffer through famine, to rescue and pray for family, and wait years and years for God's promise to be fulfilled. Now he is asked to give up his most precious possession. Grossly unfair of God to do this, we might think. Totally unreasonable.

But such is the mystery of our faith. An even greater mystery is how God the Father could place his Son, the Lord Jesus Christ, on the cross at Calvary and sacrifice him for our sins. Without his sacrifice, we are doomed. Without obedience to God, we soon slip away from our faith commitment. Abraham learns anew that God always provides a way for his people.

**1.** Of what value is the testing of our faith (see 1 Peter 1:6-7)?

**Read Genesis 22:1-14.**

♦ **2.** What did God tell Abraham to do (verses 1-2)? Why?

**3.** Put yourself in Abraham's situation. What emotions and conflicting facts about God and his promises might you struggle with?

**4.** Abraham obeyed, apparently without any dialogue with the Lord. What does this tell us about the growth of his faith and his understanding of God?

Imagine his thoughts and prayers during the three-day journey to Moriah.

♦ **5.** What clues do we have that apparently Abraham thought God would intervene (verses 5-8)? (See also Hebrews 11:17-19.)

◆ **6.** To what extent was Abraham willing to go in following the Lord (verses 9-11)?

**7.** How did the angel of the Lord explain the purpose of this test of Abraham's faith and obedience (verse 12)?

Why do you think the price was so high?

◆ **8.** What sacrifice did Abraham offer instead of Isaac (verse 13)?

Why did he give the place a special name (verses 8, 14)?

**9.** In what ways has God provided for you in times of loss or pain?

Read Genesis 22:15-19.

**10.** How did the Lord respond to Abraham's obedience (verses 15-18)?

Why was it necessary to reaffirm these promises yet again?

**11.** What is the connection between Abraham's faith and obedience and God's blessing of all nations?

What issues are at stake in our families, communities, and the world when we decide whether or not to do what God wants us to do?

**12.** Think about the cost of faith and obedience in your life. What things are we, as followers of Christ, called to lay on the altar of sacrifice? What promises of God can you claim (see Luke 18:28-30)?

# A FATHER PROVIDES FOR HIS SON

Genesis 24

Most parents hope and pray that their children will make wise choices as they begin to date and marry. Ultimately, of course, the decisions are theirs, and we commit them to God. But in Abraham's day, as in some cultures still today, arranged marriages were the tradition. Abraham's task in finding a bride for Isaac presented one more test of his faith. But he did not waver. In this beautiful story, we discover that Abraham chose the more difficult way of faith rather than make an unwise choice for his son.

**1.** How can our faith and trust in God influence our dating choices? Our choice of a life partner? Our being single?

**Read Genesis 24.**

♦ **2.** From this story, how would you describe Abraham's spiritual and material welfare?

♦ **3.** How did Abraham go about providing a wife for his son?

What alternatives did he have?

**4.** In what ways did Abraham's faith shape his approach to this crucial matter (verses 6-9)?

What role did God's covenant play in his thinking and planning?

◆ **5.** Why did Abraham extract this strong oath from his servant (verses 1-4)?

What additional condition did he attach (verses 6, 8-9)?

**6.** As the story unfolds, how do you see Abraham's faith influencing the work and words of his servant?

What do you think he did in everyday life to have such a profound influence on his servant?

**7.** What evidence do we have of the servant's own faith (verses 26-27, 48, 52)?

56

♦ 8. Identify the relatives he finds in Mesopotamia, and determine their relationship to Abraham. (See also Genesis 22:20-23.)

**9.** What kind of people were they? Describe the character qualities they exhibited.

**10.** Considering the sensitive situation he faced, how did Abraham's servant maintain his fidelity to God and to Abraham (verses 34-54)?

**11.** Think about all the different people in the story and how many delicate decisions they had to make. In what specific details did God honor Abraham's faith in this matter?

**12.** Although our customs for marriage are different than in Abraham's day, how can our commitment to God's good and perfect will affect our thinking about this crucial decision?

What steps of faith do parents have to take when their children get ready to marry?

**13.** Reflect on Abraham's spiritual maturity and confidence in the Lord. How do you account for his clearcut avoidance of Canaanite women and his confidence that God would guide his servant?

# THE DEATHS OF SARAH AND ABRAHAM

Genesis 23; 25:1-11

A friend of mine recently passed away. He did not die an old man, "full of years." Jeff was thirty-eight and left behind a wife and two young children. But in my book, Jeff stood as tall as Abraham. Throughout three years of suffering, he never gave up and quit, and he never got mad at God.

More than anything else, death forces us to come to terms with what we believe about God. Abraham and Sarah's deaths do not rate much space in the Genesis account. We are left to read subsequent prophets and New Testament writers to give Abraham his due. But the end of their lives of faith can help us reflect on our own.

**1.** Think about someone who has recently died. How would you summarize her or his life in terms of faith?

Read Genesis 23.

**2.** What problem confronted Abraham after Sarah's death (verses 3-4)?

How did he propose to solve it?

♦ **3.** How did the Hittites regard Abraham (verse 6)?

Based on our study of Abraham's life, how do you think he had gained this reputation among them?

♦ **4.** What did they offer him (verses 6, 11)?

Why do you think Abraham refused their offer and insisted on paying for the land?

**5.** Why do you think Abraham had never bothered to buy land for himself (see Hebrews 11:9-10; Acts 7:5)?

**6.** In what ways did God keep his promises to Abraham and honor Abraham's faithfulness?

---

### Read Genesis 25:1-11.

♦ **7.** In this last notice of Abraham, what facts does the writer bring together?

♦ **8.** How was Abraham's death summarized (verse 8)?

What does the expression "he was gathered to his people" mean? What does it tell us about death and dying?

**9.** How had Abraham acted in accordance with God's covenant? How did God keep his word (verses 5, 11)?

♦ **10.** There is no eulogy written for Abraham. Had you been the historian, what would you have written?

**11.** Thinking back over Abraham's life, how would you summarize what he thought about God?

**12.** If you were charting Abraham's spiritual pilgrimage on a graph, what would the high points be? the low points?

How does his journey encourage your own walk of faith?

**13.** In what ways did Abraham deserve to be called "God's friend" (see 2 Chronicles 20:7)? Why is such a name a worthy aspiration?

# THE MODEL OF SALVATION BY FAITH

Romans 4

New Testament references to Abraham abound. The Christian Gospel of salvation originated in Jewish soil. Jesus claimed to be the promised Messiah of the Jews. However, when he made that claim, the leaders and most people rejected him, saying that Abraham was their father. They could not extricate themselves from their physical and spiritual ancestor.

But God ushered in a remarkable fulfillment of his covenant promises to Abraham when he raised Jesus from the dead. Suddenly, Abraham's descendants were not his physical progeny, but his spiritual children. In this study, we will see how the apostle Paul holds up Abraham as an example of the overwhelming fact that God accepts people on the basis of their faith, not their physical descent or good works. He is our model of salvation by faith, not because he was perfect, but because he believed God's promises.

1. Many people hope that when they stand before God after they die, their good deeds will outweigh their bad ones. How would you respond to this?

---

**Read Romans 4:1-8.**

◆ **2.** To what subject did Paul refer in verses 1-3 (refer to Romans 3:21-22, 28)?

Why was this a shocking idea to the Jewish Christians to whom Paul was speaking?

◆ **3.** Why did Paul use Abraham as an example to prove his point?

◆ **4.** When it comes to being justified (declared righteous) by God, what alternatives do we have?

What is the difference between works and faith (verses 4-5)?

**5.** What works could Abraham have boasted about (verse 2)? For what did he believe God (verse 3)?

**Read Romans 4:9-17.**

♦ **6.** What crucial point did Abraham's faith and subsequent circumcision prove (verses 9-11)?

For the circumcised (Jews), what was the critical issue here (verse 12)?

♦ **7.** How does law-keeping cancel salvation by faith (verses 13-15)?

**8.** On what basis is God's promise received (verse 16)? Why?

♦ 9. Who qualifies to be Abraham's offspring (verses 16-17)?

Why is that important for non-Jews?

## Read Romans 4:18-25.

♦ 10. What facts about Abraham did Paul add to the Genesis story (verses 20-21)?

11. Paul took dead aim on Jewish legalism and salvation by works. Why is it so hard to give up the idea that we can be good enough to please God?

How does Abraham's example help us to believe, "against all hope," in what God has promised?

♦ **12.** How is righteousness before God attained today (verse 24)? On what facts do we anchor our faith (verse 25)?

**13.** Go back over the entire chapter and review the times you find the word "faith" related to Abraham. God is the other side of the faith transaction. What have you learned about God in this study of Abraham's life that strengthens your faith?

# LEADER'S NOTES

■ Study 1/A Radical Call

**Question 2.** Abram was born around 1950 B.C. He and his family migrated from Ur in southern Mesopotamia northwestward to Haran, en route to Canaan (see the map on page 6). Ur was a highly civilized city boasting of rich commerce and high culture, rivaling that of Babylon itself. Haran was the district of Abram's ancestors Peleg, Serug, Nahor, and Terah (Genesis 11:18-26). The major deity of Ur was Nannar, who was also worshiped at Haran.

**Question 4.** God's promises (later called his covenant) form the backbone of Abram's story throughout Genesis. Specific provisions of this covenant affected his son, Isaac, and his grandson Jacob. God made promises through Abram to the nation of Israel, to the future church, and to Gentile nations. Christians see the covenant as a promise that the Messiah, the Lord Jesus Christ, would descend from the family of Abram (fulfilled in Matthew 1:1-2).

**Question 9.** Abram's life was directed by personal appearances of and conversations with God. We do not have precise physical details about these appearances. Scholars call them *theophanies,* or preincarnate appearances of God the Son in either angelic or human form.

**Question 10.** Abram's altar at Shechem implies animal sacrifices. The name *Bethel* means "house of God." *Negev* means "south," referring to the barren, 4,500-square mile area between Beersheba and the Gulf of Aqaba. However, there was pasture for the flocks of nomads.

## ■ Study 2/Unexpected Roadblocks

**Question 2.** During times of famine it was customary for the peoples of Syria and Canaan to go to Egypt for food.

**Question 3.** Abram's proposal was partial truth, because Sarai was his half-sister (Genesis 20:12). Nevertheless, his purpose was to deceive. See a similar episode in the life of Isaac in Genesis 26:1-16. Sarai's beauty at age sixty-five seems remarkable. However, since she lived to be 127, her sixties would be barely middle age, the same as our thirties or forties.

**Question 8.** This dispute was the first threat to God's promise to give the land to Abram.

**Question 9.** As the younger man, Lot was expected to give Abram first choice. But Abram surrendered his rights to his nephew.

**Question 12.** The name *Mamre* means "fatness" and *Hebron* means "fellowship"(Genesis 13:18).

## ■ Study 3/Faith Takes Action

**Question 2.** In addition to nomadic life in Abram's time, many people lived in villages called walled "cities," ruled by local sheiks who were vassals of more powerful kings. Archaeologists have discovered the ruins of the ancient fortified towns mentioned in Genesis 14:5.

**Question 3.** The name *Hebrew* is used for the first time in Genesis 14:13. It means "migrant" and may be derived from "Eber," one of Abram's ancestors (Genesis 10:25).

**Question 5.** Melchizedek is also mentioned in Psalm 110:4, Hebrews 5:6, 10; 6:20; and 7:1-21. We know nothing about him historically, except that he was both king and priest in Salem (Jerusalem). However, he is seen to be a forerunner of the type of priesthood of Jesus Christ, which was superior to that of the priesthood of Aaron.

**Question 6.** "God Most High" (*El Elyon* in Hebrew) speaks of God as the owner and possessor of the universe—the world and everything in it.

**Question 8.** Abram realized that God was the Most High and did not need earthly gains. Abram gave one-tenth of his spoils not because he felt that was all he needed to give, but as a sign that he believed all of his possessions really belonged to God. This is the first recorded instance of offering a tenth of one's first fruits to God, what we call the *tithe* (see also Nehemiah 13:12 and Malachi 3:10).

### ■ Study 4/Abram's Faith Encouraged

**Question 4.** Abram used "Sovereign Lord" in Genesis 15:2, which is "Lord God" in other translations. The Hebrew word is *Adonai* meaning "Master." This indicates that Abram had learned to trust

God so that he was willing to be his slave. *Adonai* also means "Husband," revealing that Abram trusted God for his love and protection.

**Question 5.** Abram's proposal of an heir through his servant was common practice for childless couples in those days. The adoption specified that if a natural son were born later on, he would automatically become the legal heir.

**Question 9.** This phrase, "credited it to him as righteousness," is the cornerstone of the Christian doctrine of salvation. The New Testament teaches that we are all sinners without any righteousness of our own. If we are to be accepted by God, we must receive the gift of his righteousness by faith. This pivotal incident in Abram's life is used in several places by the apostle Paul. In Romans 4, Paul refers to Abraham to show that salvation is by faith, not by our good works. In Galatians 3:6, Paul shows that we continue in our Christian life by faith. And James 2:21-24 uses Abram's example to discuss how saving faith shows itself in action, as it did in Abram's case when he offered Isaac on the altar (Genesis 22).

**Question 12.** God confirmed his promise by prescribing a covenant ritual (also later referred to in Jeremiah 34:18). By killing and dividing the animals, the parties to the covenant signified that the penalty for breaking it was death. In this case, God put only himself on oath by passing between the pieces. God's presence was demonstrated by darkness, smoke, and fire, as it was at Sinai when he gave the Ten Commandments (see Exodus 19:18 and Hebrews 12:18).

### ■ Study 5/When Faith Can't Wait

**Question 2.** It was customary for childless women to give slave girls to their husbands. This was written into the marriage contract. Children born to slave girls would then belong to the wife.

**Question 6.** Ancient law codes prescribed punishment if a pregnant female slave claimed equality with her mistress.

**Question 10.** The name *Ishmael* means "God shall hear." The well called Beer Lahai Roi ("well of the Living One who sees me") near Kadesh indicates that Hagar had wandered quite a distance into the wilderness.

## ■ Study 6/A New Covenant

**Question 3.** "God Almighty" comes from the Hebrew name *El Shaddai*. This was the name for God commonly used by the patriarchs before the giving of the law at Mount Sinai. *El Shaddai* signifies God as the strength and satisfaction of his people, who enriches them and makes them fruitful.

**Question 6.** In Abram's day names carried importance and prestige, often referring to one's status in family, society, and religion. In the Bible, issues of faith and salvation are connected to the meaning of names. Abram's new relationship with God merited a new name. Later on, God gave Jacob a new name also.

**Question 8.** There is evidence that circumcision was already practiced in ancient Egypt, but not in Canaan and Babylon. Genesis 17 does not tell its origin, but how God prescribed it for Abraham and his descendants to show their unique covenant relationship with him.

**Question 11.** The apostle Paul explains how this sign of the covenant is now applied to Christians. See Romans 4:11-12, Galatians 5:6, and Colossians 2:11-12.

## ◼ Study 7/A Bold Prayer

**Question 2.** One of the three men apparently was the LORD, the preincarnate Son of God, and the other two were angels, who appear later in Sodom (Genesis 19:1).

**Question 6.** Traditional Middle Eastern religion taught that the wickedness of the few contaminated the whole. Abraham took the opposite approach.

**Question 7.** God is love and God is holy. Because he loves justice, God judges according to truth. Thus his judgments are impartial and not vindictive.

## ◼ Study 8/A Son Is Born

**Question 2.** For historical context, you may want to summarize for the group Genesis 19–20. In Genesis 19, God's judgment overtook Sodom and Gomorrah. Meanwhile, in Genesis 20 we see a reprise of Abraham's earlier downfall in Egypt (see Genesis 12:10-20). Abraham and Sarah tried to deceive Abimelech, but failed. In spite of this failure, God's grace intervened once again. As Genesis 21 opens, twenty-five years have passed between the giving of God's promise of a son and its fulfillment.

**Question 9.** In biblical terms, faith means believing and receiving what God has revealed. It is trust in the God of the Scriptures and in Jesus Christ whom he has sent. By faith we receive Jesus as Lord and Savior. Faith gives rise to loving obedience and good works.

**Question 10.** Sarah's demand that Abraham send Hagar and Ishmael away ran counter to custom. Abraham needed a word from

God before he was willing to do it. Galatians 4:22-31 shows why the rift was inevitable.

**Question 11.** Ishmael was by now about sixteen years old. Isaac would have been two or three by the time he was weaned.

## ■ Study 9/Abraham's Severest Test

**Question 2.** Abraham's life was marked by four costly surrenders: (1) leaving his country and kinsmen; (2) separation from his nephew Lot; (3) abandoning his plans for Ishmael; (4) yielding his son Isaac. In the case of Isaac, God tested Abraham's sincerity, loyalty, and faith. God does not solicit people to do evil (James 1:2, 13-14).

The region of Moriah (which means "bitter") was one of the hills on which Jerusalem now stands. Some say it was the site of Solomon's temple (2 Chronicles 3:1). The fifty-mile journey took him three days.

**Question 5.** There is a striking parallel between Abraham's sacrifice and the greater sacrifice of God's own Son. However, the writer of Hebrews draws the lesson of faith from this incident.

**Question 6.** Though we don't know his exact age, Isaac was probably a young man by this time, not a child.

**Question 8.** God's saving love for humanity is revealed in various compound names for God in Scripture, such as "The Lord Will Provide" (*Jehovah-jireh*). This name reflected Abraham's faith (Genesis 22:8), and became a proverb among the Jews (Genesis 22:14), who said that as God provided for Abraham in his great need, so he would provide for them.

## ■ Study 10/A Father Provides for His Son

**Question 2.** When this story begins, Abraham is dwelling comfortably in Beersheba (Genesis 22:19). Also, Sarah, his beloved wife, has died. We will look at her death and burial in Study 11.

**Question 3.** This is one of the most beautiful stories in the Old Testament. It reflects the traditional arranged marriage in Middle Eastern culture of that time.

**Question 5.** Placing the hand under the thigh was an ancient ritual for confirming an oath. Abraham's concern here was not racial but religious. His great fear was loss of faith in the one true God and the influence of Canaanite idolatrous religions. (See Exodus 34:15-16 and Deuteronomy 7:3-4).

**Question 8.** The area called Aram Naharaim was in central Mesopotamia. The town of Nahor was near Haran, the city where Abraham had settled before God's call (Genesis 11:27-31). "The city of Nahor could mean either the place of that name, or more probably merely the city where Abraham's brother lived" (*Tyndale Old Testament Commentary Series,* "Genesis," Derek Kidner, p. 147, Downers Grove, Ill: InterVarsity Press, 1967). Nahor and Milcah were Abraham's brother and sister-in-law (Genesis 22:20-24).

## ■ Study 11/The Deaths of Sarah and Abraham

**Question 3.** The Hebrew word for "mighty prince" literally means "prince with God."

**Question 4.** The shekel was a piece of silver, not a coin. Minted coins before 700 B.C. have not been found in Bible lands. Mention of shekels in earlier stories refers to weights, not coins. The transaction conformed to known Hittite laws, including the trees, the weighing of silver, and the witnesses. Family tombs usually were caves or holes cut from rock. The traditional site of Abraham and Sarah's burial in Hebron is now covered by a mosque.

**Question 7.** Abraham lived thirty-eight years after Sarah's death. His physical powers were renewed by the Lord.

**Question 8.** The expression "gathered to his people" implies life after death, reflecting continuity, not the end.

**Question 10.** The New Testament honors Abraham as God's friend (James 2:23), as our spiritual father (Romans 4:11; Galatians 3:7), as an illustration of justification by faith (Romans 4), and as an illustration of what it means to live by faith (Hebrews 11:8-19).

### ■ Study 12/The Model of Salvation by Faith

**Question 2.** The terms *justification* and *righteousness* are translations of similar Greek words, meaning "to declare righteous, to justify." Believers are justified, that is, declared and treated as righteous by God, on the basis of Christ's atoning death.

**Question 3.** The Jews believed that if anybody was considered righteous, it was Abraham. The question was, on what grounds did God count him as righteous? His works or his faith? Paul backed his claim from holy Scripture, referring to Genesis 15:6.

**Question 4.** God's work in response to Abraham's faith is described eleven times in this chapter by the words "credited," "credits," and "count." The same Greek word is used each time. It means "to put to one's account." God reckons believing sinners righteous, then gives them his own righteousness, Christ himself.

78

**Question 6.** The sign of circumcision was given to Abraham when he was ninety-nine years old (Genesis 17:10). He was counted righteous by God about fifteen years before that (Genesis 15:6). Therefore, Paul proved that an outward sign had nothing to do with God's counting him as righteous.

**Question 7.** Faith, and not law, was the basis of God's promise to Abraham and his posterity. Compare Galatians 3:16-18.

**Question 9.** The reference in Romans 4:17 is to Genesis 17:5.

**Question 10.** Abraham is still the subject in Romans 4:18. Paul quotes Genesis 15:5.

**Question 12.** The Lord Jesus Christ was raised from the dead, after he had been crucified for our sins, as a sign that God accepted his death as the payment of the penalty.

# WHAT SHOULD WE STUDY NEXT?

To help your group answer that question, we've listed the Fisherman Guides by category so you can choose your next study.

## TOPICAL STUDIES

**Angels,** Wright
**Becoming Women of Purpose,** Barton
**Building Your House on the Lord,** Brestin
**The Creative Heart of God,** Goring
**Discipleship,** Reapsome
**Doing Justice, Showing Mercy,** Wright
**Encouraging Others,** Johnson
**The End Times,** Rusten
**Examining the Claims of Jesus,** Brestin
**Friendship,** Brestin
**The Fruit of the Spirit,** Briscoe
**Great Doctrines of the Bible,** Board
**Great Passages of the Bible,** Plueddemann
**Great Prayers of the Bible,** Plueddemann
**Growing Through Life's Challenges,** Reapsome
**Guidance & God's Will,** Stark
**Heart Renewal,** Goring
**Higher Ground,** Brestin
**Images of Redemption,** Van Reken

**Integrity,** Engstrom & Larson
**Lifestyle Priorities,** White
**Marriage,** Stevens
**Miracles,** Castleman
**One Body, One Spirit,** Larsen
**The Parables of Jesus,** Hunt
**Prayer,** Jones
**The Prophets,** Wright
**Proverbs & Parables,** Brestin
**Satisfying Work,** Stevens & Schoberg
**Senior Saints,** Reapsome
**Sermon on the Mount,** Hunt
**Spiritual Gifts,** Dockrey
**A Spiritual Legacy,** Christensen
**Spiritual Warfare,** Moreau
**The Ten Commandments,** Briscoe
**Ultimate Hope for Changing Times,** Larsen
**Who Is God?** Seemuth
**Who Is Jesus?** Van Reken
**Who Is the Holy Spirit?** Knuckles & Van Reken
**Wisdom for Today's Woman: Insights from Esther,** Smith
**Witnesses to All the World,** Plueddemann
**Women at Midlife,** Miley
**Worship,** Sibley

# BIBLE BOOK STUDIES

Genesis, Fromer & Keyes
Exodus, Larsen
Job, Klug
Psalms, Klug
Proverbs: Wisdom That Works,
  Wright
Jeremiah, Reapsome
Jonah, Habakkuk, & Malachi,
  Fromer & Keyes
Matthew, Sibley
Mark, Christensen
Luke, Keyes
John: Living Word, Kuniholm
Acts 1-12, Christensen
Paul (Acts 13-28), Christiansen
Romans: The Christian
  Story, Reapsome
1 Corinthians, Hummel

Strengthened to Serve
  (2 Corinthians),
  Plueddemann
Galatians, Titus & Philemon,
  Kuniholm
Ephesians, Baylis
Philippians, Klug
Colossians, Shaw
Letters to the Thessalonians,
  Fromer & Keyes
Letters to Timothy, Fromer &
  Keyes
Hebrews, Hunt
James, Christensen
1 & 2 Peter, Jude, Brestin
How Should a Christian Live?
  (1, 2 & 3 John), Brestin
Revelation, Hunt

# BIBLE CHARACTER STUDIES

David: Man after God's Own
  Heart, Castleman
Elijah, Castleman
Great People of the Bible,
  Plueddemann
King David: Trusting God for
  a Lifetime, Castleman
Men Like Us, Heidebrecht &
  Scheuermann

Moses, Asimakoupoulos
Paul (Acts 13-28), Christensen
Women Like Us, Barton
Women Who Achieved for
  God, Christensen
Women Who Believed God,
  Christensen

Printed in the United States
by Baker & Taylor Publisher Services